~A BINGO BOOK~

New Hampshire Bingo Book

COMPLETE BINGO GAME IN A BOOK

Written By Rebecca Stark

ISBN 978-0-87386-522-7

Educational Books 'n' Bingo

Printed in the U.S.A.

DIRECTIONS

INCLUDED:

List of Terms

Templates for Additional Terms and Clues

2 Clues per Term

30 Unique Bingo Cards

Markers

1. **Either cut apart the book or make copies of ALL the sheets. You might want to make an extra copy of the clue sheets to use for introduction and review. Keep the sheets in an envelope for easy reuse.**

2. Cut apart the call cards with terms and clues.

3. Pass out one bingo card per student. There are enough for a class of 30.

4. Pass out markers. You may cut apart the markers included in this book or use any other small items of your choice.

5. Decide whether or not you will require the entire card to be filled. Requiring the entire card to be filled provides a better review. However, if you have a short time to fill, you may prefer to have them do the just the border or some other format. Tell the class before you begin what is required.

6. There are 50 terms. Read the list before you begin. If there are any terms that have not been covered in class, you may want to read to the students the term and clues before you begin.

7. There is a blank space in the middle of each card. You can instruct the students to use it as a free space or you can write in answers to cover terms not included. Of course, in this case you would create your own clues. (Templates provided.)

8. Shuffle the cards and place them in a pile. Two or three clues are provided for each term. If you plan to play the game with the same group more than once, you might want to choose a different clue for each game. If not, you may choose to use more than one clue.

9. Be sure to keep the cards you have used for the present game in a separate pile. When a student calls, "Bingo," he or she will have to verify that the correct answers are on his or her card AND that the markers were placed in response to the proper questions. Pull out the cards that are on the student's card keeping them in the order they were used in the game. Read each clue as it was given and ask the student to identify the correct answer from his or her card.

10. If the student has the correct answers on the card AND has shown that they were marked in response to the *correct questions,* then that student is the winner and the game is over. If the student does not have the correct answers on the card OR he or she marked the answers in response to *the wrong questions,* then the game continues until there is a proper winner.

11. If you want to play again, reshuffle the cards and begin again.

Have fun!

TERMS INCLUDED

Agricultural

American Independence Museum

Apple(s)

Beryl

Flower

Border (-ed)

Chinook

Climate

Coastal Lowlands

Concord

County (-ies)

Eastern New England Upland

Executive Branch

Fish

Flag

Fort William and Mary

Gilman

Granite

Independence

Insect

Judicial Branch

Lake(s)

Legislature

Manchester

Merrimack River

Mine (-ed)

Motto

Mount Washington

Nashua

New Castle

New England

Franklin Pierce

Portsmouth

Primary

Purple Finch (-es)

Quarter

Quartz

River(s)

Seal

Shipbuilding

Skiing

Song(s)

Spotted Newt

John Stark

Tribes

Union

Daniel Webster

White Birch

White Mountains

White-tail Deer

Additional Terms

Choose as many additional terms as you would like and write them in the squares. Repeat each as desired.
Cut out the squares and randomly distribute them to the class.
Instruct the students to place their square on the center space of their card.

New Hampshire Bingo

Clues for
Additional Terms

Write three clues for each of your additional terms.

_____	_____
1.	1.
2.	2.
3.	3.
_____	_____
1.	1.
2.	2.
3.	3.
_____	_____
1.	1.
2.	2.
3.	3.

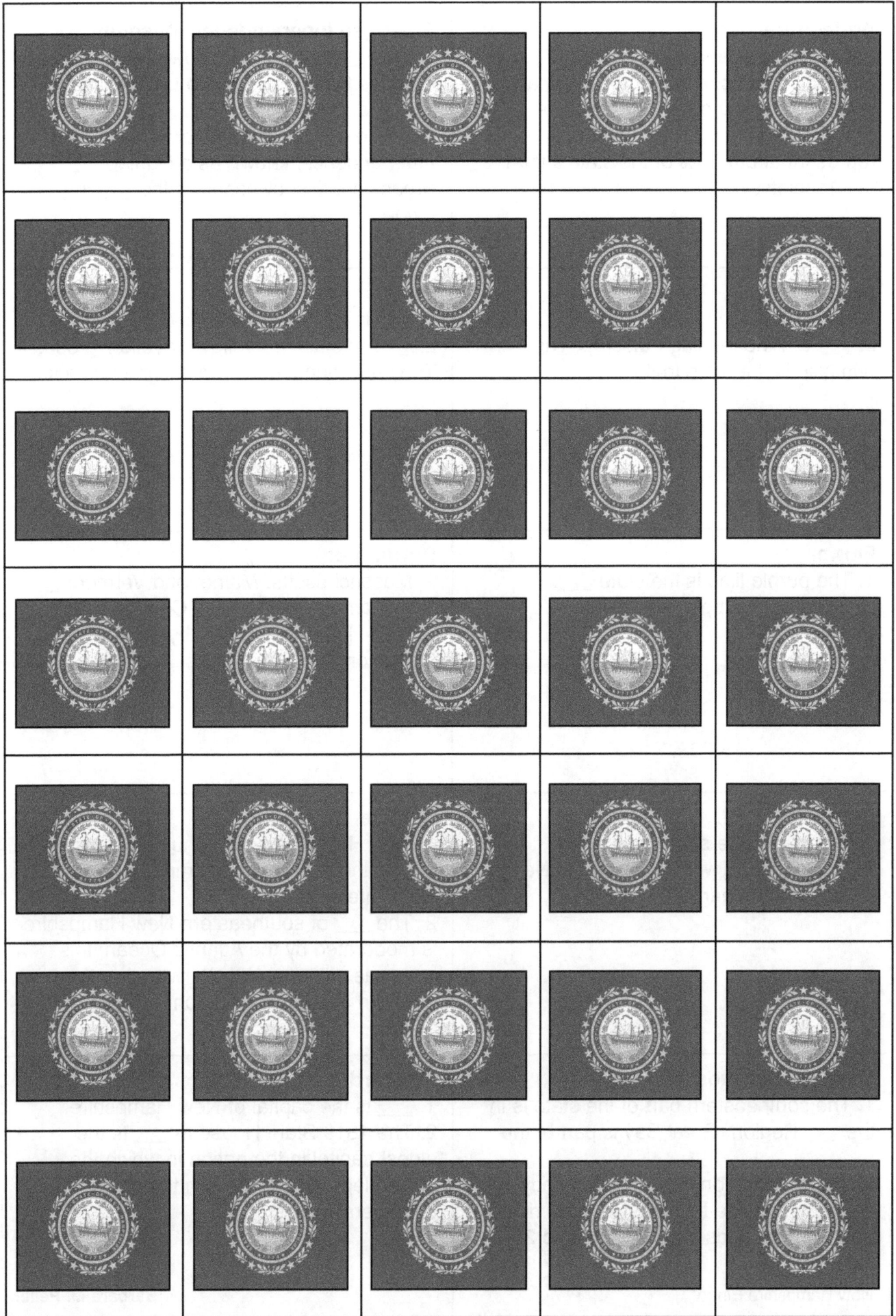

Agricultural 1. Greenhouse and nursery products, dairy products, apples, cattle and calves, and sweet corn are the top ___ products. 2. Dairy farming and dairy products represent about 30% of the state's total ___ receipts.	**American Independence Museum** 1. The ___ is in historic downtown Exeter. It includes two buildings: the Ladd-Gilman House and the Folsom Tavern. 2. A rare copy of the *Declaration of Independence,* known as a Dunlap Broadside, is showcased at the ___ in Exeter.
Apple(s) 1. ___ cider is the state beverage. 2. ___ are the leading fruit crop. The pumpkin is the state fruit.	**Beryl** 1. ___ is the state mineral. 2. ___ crystals are yellow or yellow-green. They are found in the state's granite rocks.
Flower 1. The purple lilac is the state ___. 2. Pink lady's slipper is the state wild___.	**Border (-ed)** 1. Massachusetts, Maine, and Vermont ___ New Hampshire. So does Canada. 2. New Hampshire is ___ by the Atlantic Ocean on the east.
Chinook 1. The ___ is the state dog. 2. This sled dog was developed in New England in the early 20th century.	**Climate** 1. New Hampshire has a humid, continental ___, with warm, humid summers and cold, wet winters. 2. The ___ of southeastern New Hampshire is moderated by the Atlantic Ocean; this area has milder and wetter weather than the northern and interior portions.
Coastal Lowlands 1. The southeastern part of the state is in the ___ Region. Great Bay is part of the ___. 2. The ___ Region includes the sandy beaches that line the coast and the rivers and tidal wetlands that extend 15 to 20 miles inland.	**Concord** 1. ___ is the capital of New Hampshire. 2. The 1819 State House in ___ is the oldest capitol in the nation in which the state's legislature meets in the original chambers.

New Hampshire Bingo

County (-ies)	Eastern New England Upland
1. There are 10 ___ in New Hampshire. 2. Hillsborough is the largest ___. It has 2 seats: Manchester and Nashua.	1. Most of southern New Hampshire is in the ___ Region. This region runs from northern Maine south to eastern Connecticut. 2. The New Hampshire section of the the ___ Region comprises 3 distinct areas: the Merrimack Valley, the Hills and Lakes Region, and the Connecticut River Valley.
Executive Branch 1. The ___ comprises the governor, an executive council, and various state agencies. 2. The governor is the head of the ___. The present-day governor is [fill in].	**Fish** 1. Brook trout is the state freshwater ___. 2. Striped bass is the state saltwater game ___.
Flag 1. The state ___ consists of the Great Seal centered on a blue field. 2. A wreath of laurel leaves surrounds the seal on the state ___. Nine stars are interspersed. They represent New Hampshire as the ninth state.	**Fort William and Mary** 1. When news arrived in December 1774 that a British warship might take possession of ___, two bands of patriots stormed the fort and removed its gunpowder and arms. 2. Some consider the gunpowder raids on ___ the first overt act of the American Revolution.
Gilman 1. This New Hampshire family included statesmen, educators, authors, architects, businessmen, and abolitionists. 2. A tour of the Ladd-___ House provides a glimpse into the lives of the ___ family between 1720 and 1820. It is a registered National Landmark.	**Granite** 1. ___ is the state rock. 2. The "__ State" is a popular nickname. It refers to the state's extensive ___ quarries.
Independence 1. New Hampshire was the first state to declare its ___ from Great Britain. 2. New Hampshire declared its ___ from Great Britain six months before the *Declaration of Independence* was signed.	**Insect** 1. The ladybug is the official state ___. 2. There are two state ___: the ladybug and the Karner blue, which is the state butterfly.

New Hampshire Bingo

Judicial Branch 1. The ___ interprets what our laws mean and makes decisions about the laws and those who break them. 2. The Supreme Court is the highest court in the ___ of the state government.	**Lake(s)** 1. Winnipesaukee, Newfound, and Squam are ___ in New Hampshire. 2. Winnipesaukee is the largest ___ in New Hampshire.
Legislature 1. The New Hampshire ___ is called the General Court. It comprises the Senate and the House of Representatives. 2. The ___ makes the laws.	**Manchester** 1. ___ is the largest city in New Hampshire. It is nicknamed "Queen City." 2. The Merrimack River divides the city of ___ into eastern and western sections.
Merrimack River 1. The Amoskeag Falls are a set of waterfalls on the ___. 2. The ___ divides the city of Manchester into eastern and western sections.	**Mine (-ed)** 1. Sand and gravel for roads and concrete are important ___ products. 2. A quarry is a type of open-pit ___ from which rock or minerals are extracted. New Hampshire's most popular nickname is the "Granite State."
Motto 1. New Hampshire's ___ is "Live Free or Die." 2. The state ___ is taken from a toast by General John Stark, a hero of the Revolutionary War.	**Mount Washington** 1. At 6,288 feet, ___ is the highest point in the state. 2. ___, the highest point in New England, is part of the Presidential Range in the White Mountains Region.
Nashua 1. ___ is the second largest city in New Hampshire. 2. ___ is located at the confluence of the Merrimack and Nashua rivers.	**New Castle** 1. Fort Constitution in ___ is the former site of Fort William and Mary. 2. Fort Stark in ___ was named in honor of the commander of New Hampshire forces at the Battle of Bennington. It is one of seven forts built to protect Portsmouth Harbor.

New Hampshire Bingo

New England
1. ___ comprises Maine, New Hampshire, Vermont, Massachusetts, Rhode Island, and Connecticut.
2. The ___ Colonies of British America included Massachusetts Bay Colony, Connecticut Colony, Colony of Rhode Island and Providence Plantations, and Province of New Hampshire.

Franklin Pierce
1. This New Hampshirite was the 14th President of the United States.
2. This President was born in Hillsborough, New Hampshire, on November 23, 1804. The ___ Homestead in Hillsborough is a National Historic Landmark.

Portsmouth
1. ___ was the colonial capital.
2. The only battle fought in New Hampshire was the raid on Fort William and Mary. It took place on December 14, 1774, in ___ Harbor.

Primary
1. Every four years New Hampshire holds the first ___ in the U.S. presidential election cycle.
2. ___ elections narrow the field of candidates before the general election.

Purple Finch (-es)
1. The ___ is the state bird.
2. Male ___ are reddish-purple except for their white bellies. The brightest coloring is on their breasts and heads.

Quarter
1. The New Hampshire quarter depicts "The Old Man of the Mountain," a rock formation on Mt. Cannon in Franconia Notch.
2. The state motto, "Live free or die," is on the state quarter.

Quartz
1. Smoky ___ is the state gem.
2. ___ is a common mineral found in many types of rocks, including granite, the state rock.

River(s)
1. The Androscoggin, Connecticut, and Merrimack are major ___ in New Hampshire.
2. The Connecticut ___ is the largest in New England.

Seal
1. The frigate *Raleigh,* built in Portsmouth for the U.S. navy in 1776, is depicted in the center of the Great ___. The year 1776 appears beneath it.
2. The Great ___ is in the center of the blue field of the state flag.

Shipbuilding
1. The ship depicted on the New Hampshire state flag represents ___.
2. ___ was important in Colonial New Hampshire. Coastal towns like Portsmouth, New Castle, Rye, Hampton, and Seabrook all participated in this trade.

New Hampshire Bingo

Skiing
1. ___ is the state sport.
2. Alpine and cross-country ___ are popular sports in New Hampshire.

Song(s)
1. There are 10 official state ___.
2. "Old New Hampshire" was the first official state ___. "Live Free or Die" was the tenth.

Spotted Newt
1. The ___ is the state amphibian.
2. The ___ is a common salamander. It lives in moist environments, such as small lakes, ponds, and streams.

John Stark
1. ___ was a Revolutionary War hero. He was a company commander with Rogers' Rangers and was a hero at both Bunker Hill and the Battle of Bennington.
2. The state's motto, "Live Free or Die," was taken from his toast at the 32nd reunion of the Battle of Bennington.

Tribes
1. The Abenaki and Pennacook ___ inhabited the area that is now New Hampshire when the Europeans arrived.
2. There are no federally recognized Native American ___ in New Hampshire today.

Union
1. New Hampshire was one of the original 13 states. It was admitted to the ___ on June 21, 1788.
2. New Hampshire was the ninth state to join the ___.

Daniel Webster
1. This lawyer, statesman, and orator was born in Salisbury, the present-day city of Franklin.
2. ___ spoke in favor of the Constitution, the federal government, and the Union. He said, "Liberty and Union, now and forever one and inseparable."

White Birch
1. The ___ is the state tree.
2. Native Americans used bark from the ___ to make canoes.

White Mountains
1. The ___ are part of the Appalachians. They are the most rugged mountains in New England.
2. The ___ are in the northern part of the state. This region consists of rugged mountains and narrow valleys. Mt. Washington, the highest point in New England, is in the ___.

White-tail Deer
1. The ___ is the state animal.
2. The ___ can run up to 40 miles per hour and swim 13 miles per hour. The white underside of the its tail waves when running and is flashed as a danger signal.

New Hampshire Bingo

New Hampshire Bingo

River(s)	Agricultural	Apple(s)	Independence	Flower
Gilman	American Independence Museum	White Birch	New Castle	Skiing
Daniel Webster	Nashua		Purple Finch (-es)	White Mountains
Union	Shipbuilding	Tribes	Mount Washington	Franklin Pierce
Primary	Lake(s)	Fish	Spotted Newt	Merrimack River

New Hampshire Bingo

Union	Daniel Webster	Manchester	Seal	Motto
Franklin Pierce	Flag	Climate	Shipbuilding	Portsmouth
Concord	Lake(s)		Legislature	Tribes
Quarter	Quartz	Nashua	White-tail Deer	Flower
Skiing	White Birch	Fish	Gilman	Spotted Newt

New Hampshire Bingo

Lake(s)	Tribes	Flag	Mount Washington	Daniel Webster
Franklin Pierce	American Independence Museum	Coastal Lowlands	Agricultural	Judicial Branch
Shipbuilding	White Birch		Portsmouth	Beryl
Nashua	Concord	Primary	Quarter	Manchester
Spotted Newt	County (-ies)	Fish	White-tail Deer	Motto

New Hampshire Bingo: Card No. 3

New Hampshire Bingo

Nashua	Portsmouth	Apple(s)	County (-ies)	Motto
New England	Chinook	Agricultural	Seal	Daniel Webster
Purple Finch (-es)	Quarter		Merrimack River	Independence
Tribes	American Independence Museum	White Birch	Fish	Climate
Eastern New England Upland	Skiing	Border (-ed)	Spotted Newt	White Mountains

New Hampshire Bingo

Skiing	Flower	Shipbuilding	Climate	County (-ies)
New England	Tribes	Coastal Lowlands	Legislature	American Independence Museum
Apple(s)	White Mountains		New Castle	Insect
Merrimack River	Motto	River(s)	White-tail Deer	Executive Branch
Flag	Fish	Daniel Webster	Nashua	Purple Finch (-es)

New Hampshire Bingo: Card No. 5

New Hampshire Bingo

Beryl	Portsmouth	Manchester	Motto	White Mountains
Mount Washington	Shipbuilding	Executive Branch	Agricultural	Daniel Webster
Seal	Eastern New England Upland		Chinook	Legislature
Fish	Primary	White-tail Deer	Border (-ed)	Apple(s)
Franklin Pierce	Climate	River(s)	Purple Finch (-es)	Fort William and Mary

New Hampshire Bingo

River(s)	Portsmouth	Insect	Tribes	Flag
Franklin Pierce	Motto	Lake(s)	American Independence Museum	New England
White Mountains	Independence		Legislature	Chinook
Nashua	Quarter	Coastal Lowlands	Union	Concord
Fish	County (-ies)	White-tail Deer	Border (-ed)	Beryl

New Hampshire Bingo

Purple Finch (-es)	Portsmouth	Granite	Mount Washington	Chinook
New England	Apple(s)	Seal	White Mountains	Climate
Fort William and Mary	County (-ies)		Motto	Flower
Spotted Newt	Nashua	Union	Eastern New England Upland	Quarter
White Birch	Fish	Border (-ed)	Shipbuilding	Franklin Pierce

New Hampshire Bingo: Card No. 8

New Hampshire Bingo

Legislature	Flag	Lake(s)	Fort William and Mary	County (-ies)
Eastern New England Upland	Motto	Purple Finch (-es)	Shipbuilding	Portsmouth
Judicial Branch	River(s)		American Independence Museum	Granite
Executive Branch	Flower	Primary	New Castle	Insect
Quarter	White-tail Deer	Coastal Lowlands	Union	Merrimack River

New Hampshire Bingo

Union	Mount Washington	Chinook	Seal	Fort William and Mary
White Mountains	Climate	Agricultural	American Independence Museum	Motto
County (-ies)	Portsmouth		Independence	Concord
Primary	Merrimack River	Executive Branch	White-tail Deer	Judicial Branch
Coastal Lowlands	Franklin Pierce	Manchester	Skiing	Purple Finch (-es)

New Hampshire Bingo

Beryl	Portsmouth	Shipbuilding	Executive Branch	Franklin Pierce
Granite	Judicial Branch	New Castle	Legislature	Agricultural
New England	Motto		Manchester	Lake(s)
Coastal Lowlands	Daniel Webster	White-tail Deer	County (-ies)	Union
Eastern New England Upland	Fish	River(s)	Border (-ed)	Flag

New Hampshire Bingo

Flag	Flower	Judicial Branch	Mount Washington	Legislature
Lake(s)	Franklin Pierce	Apple(s)	Border (-ed)	American Independence Museum
River(s)	Insect		White Mountains	Seal
Fish	Quarter	Motto	Union	New England
Portsmouth	Granite	County (-ies)	Eastern New England Upland	Climate

New Hampshire Bingo: Card No. 12

New Hampshire Bingo

Executive Branch	Flower	Beryl	Judicial Branch	White Mountains
Apple(s)	Granite	Motto	Legislature	Concord
Mount Washington	Climate		Lake(s)	Insect
Purple Finch (-es)	White-tail Deer	Chinook	County (-ies)	Union
Fish	Merrimack River	Border (-ed)	River(s)	New Castle

New Hampshire Bingo

Gilman	Motto	Shipbuilding	Legislature	Eastern New England Upland
Climate	River(s)	Judicial Branch	American Independence Museum	Portsmouth
Executive Branch	Independence		Manchester	Coastal Lowlands
Merrimack River	White-tail Deer	County (-ies)	Chinook	Beryl
Fish	Seal	Concord	Franklin Pierce	Purple Finch (-es)

New Hampshire Bingo

New Castle	Legislature	Shipbuilding	Flag	Mount Washington
Beryl	Manchester	Agricultural	Apple(s)	Eastern New England Upland
White Mountains	River(s)		Daniel Webster	Portsmouth
Fish	Judicial Branch	Granite	White-tail Deer	Executive Branch
Franklin Pierce	Quarter	Border (-ed)	Fort William and Mary	Lake(s)

New Hampshire Bingo

Chinook	Judicial Branch	Granite	Fort William and Mary	Quartz
Seal	Concord	Insect	New England	Independence
Executive Branch	Flower		White Mountains	Lake(s)
Nashua	Climate	Fish	New Castle	Union
Eastern New England Upland	John Stark	Border (-ed)	Quarter	Portsmouth

New Hampshire Bingo: Card No. 16

New Hampshire Bingo

Coastal Lowlands	Song(s)	Mine (-ed)	Judicial Branch	Gilman
New Castle	Eastern New England Upland	White-tail Deer	Independence	Insect
Legislature	Purple Finch (-es)		John Stark	Granite
Merrimack River	Franklin Pierce	Union	Shipbuilding	Concord
Primary	Executive Branch	Flag	Mount Washington	Flower

New Hampshire Bingo: Card No. 17

New Hampshire Bingo

Fort William and Mary	County (-ies)	Climate	Executive Branch	Seal
Portsmouth	Coastal Lowlands	Primary	White Mountains	Eastern New England Upland
Legislature	Concord		Mine (-ed)	Apple(s)
Flower	Agricultural	White-tail Deer	Union	Manchester
John Stark	Judicial Branch	Shipbuilding	Song(s)	Beryl

New Hampshire Bingo: Card No. 18

New Hampshire Bingo

White Mountains	Beryl	Judicial Branch	Granite	Union
New Castle	Mount Washington	Portsmouth	Flag	Independence
Song(s)	County (-ies)		American Independence Museum	Daniel Webster
Manchester	John Stark	Primary	Quarter	Mine (-ed)
Apple(s)	Quartz	Franklin Pierce	Purple Finch (-es)	Border (-ed)

New Hampshire Bingo

Gilman	Song(s)	Mount Washington	Judicial Branch	Border (-ed)
Climate	Lake(s)	New England	Primary	Seal
Flower	Insect		Nashua	Agricultural
Skiing	White Birch	Spotted Newt	Quarter	John Stark
Tribes	Purple Finch (-es)	Quartz	Union	Mine (-ed)

New Hampshire Bingo

New Castle	Beryl	New England	Judicial Branch	Skiing
Flower	Mine (-ed)	Chinook	Granite	River(s)
Concord	Franklin Pierce		Song(s)	Shipbuilding
Primary	Flag	John Stark	Merrimack River	Purple Finch (-es)
Nashua	Quartz	Border (-ed)	Coastal Lowlands	Quarter

New Hampshire Bingo

Fort William and Mary	Manchester	Mine (-ed)	Apple(s)	Executive Branch
Seal	Mount Washington	Daniel Webster	Granite	American Independence Museum
Climate	Independence		River(s)	Insect
John Stark	Merrimack River	Quarter	Agricultural	New England
Quartz	Coastal Lowlands	Song(s)	Concord	Nashua

New Hampshire Bingo: Card No. 22

© Barbara M. Peller

New Hampshire Bingo

Chinook	Song(s)	Flag	Apple(s)	Border (-ed)
Beryl	Gilman	Franklin Pierce	New Castle	Agricultural
Manchester	Executive Branch		Spotted Newt	River(s)
Concord	Quartz	John Stark	Coastal Lowlands	Quarter
Skiing	White Birch	Purple Finch (-es)	Primary	Mine (-ed)

New Hampshire Bingo

Chinook	Purple Finch (-es)	Gilman	Song(s)	Granite
Mine (-ed)	Border (-ed)	New England	Seal	River(s)
Insect	Fort William and Mary		Executive Branch	Concord
Skiing	Spotted Newt	John Stark	Coastal Lowlands	Flower
Tribes	Nashua	Quartz	Mount Washington	White Birch

New Hampshire Bingo: Card No. 24

New Hampshire Bingo

Nashua	New England	Song(s)	Shipbuilding	Mine (-ed)
Agricultural	Flower	New Castle	Chinook	American Independence Museum
Merrimack River	Granite		Spotted Newt	John Stark
Daniel Webster	Skiing	White Birch	Quartz	Independence
Border (-ed)	Gilman	Climate	Eastern New England Upland	Tribes

New Hampshire Bingo

Mine (-ed)	Song(s)	Manchester	Seal	Fort William and Mary
Primary	Mount Washington	Granite	Gilman	Chinook
Merrimack River	Spotted Newt		Independence	Nashua
Coastal Lowlands	Apple(s)	Skiing	Quartz	John Stark
Insect	Eastern New England Upland	Shipbuilding	White Birch	Tribes

New Hampshire Bingo

Manchester	Climate	Song(s)	Gilman	Lake(s)
Skiing	Spotted Newt	New Castle	John Stark	American Independence Museum
White-tail Deer	White Birch		Quartz	Nashua
Fort William and Mary	Beryl	New England	Tribes	Agricultural
Eastern New England Upland	Independence	Mine (-ed)	Daniel Webster	Insect

New Hampshire Bingo

Manchester	Gilman	Daniel Webster	Song(s)	Chinook
Lake(s)	Mine (-ed)	Spotted Newt	Seal	Independence
White Birch	Concord		Insect	Primary
Union	Fort William and Mary	Franklin Pierce	Quartz	John Stark
Apple(s)	Legislature	Eastern New England Upland	Tribes	Skiing

© Barbara M. Peller

New Hampshire Bingo

Mine (-ed)	Gilman	Fort William and Mary	New Castle	Legislature
Quarter	Primary	New England	Insect	Daniel Webster
Merrimack River	Spotted Newt		American Independence Museum	Song(s)
Lake(s)	Skiing	Motto	Quartz	John Stark
Chinook	Granite	Tribes	Beryl	White Birch

New Hampshire Bingo: Card No. 29

New Hampshire Bingo

County (-ies)	Song(s)	Seal	Legislature	John Stark
Agricultural	Gilman	Manchester	Independence	American Independence Museum
Merrimack River	Executive Branch		Insect	New England
Tribes	Beryl	Apple(s)	Quartz	Spotted Newt
Skiing	White Mountains	White Birch	Mine (-ed)	Daniel Webster

www.ingramcontent.com/pod-product-compliance
Lightning Source LLC
LaVergne TN
LVHW061341060426
835511LV00014B/2055